SADIE'S BIRTHDAY COLORING BOOK
KIDS PERSONALIZED BOOKS

Have our elves create a personalized book with the name of your choice today!

VISIT US AT:
PersonalizeThisBook.com

All rights reserved. No part of this book may be reproduced or transmitted in any form by any means, electronic or mechanical, including photocopying, scanning and recording, or by any information storage and retrieval system, without permission in writing from the publisher, except for the review for inclusion in a magazine , newpaper or broadcast.

Cover and page design by Cool Journals Studios - Copyright 2017

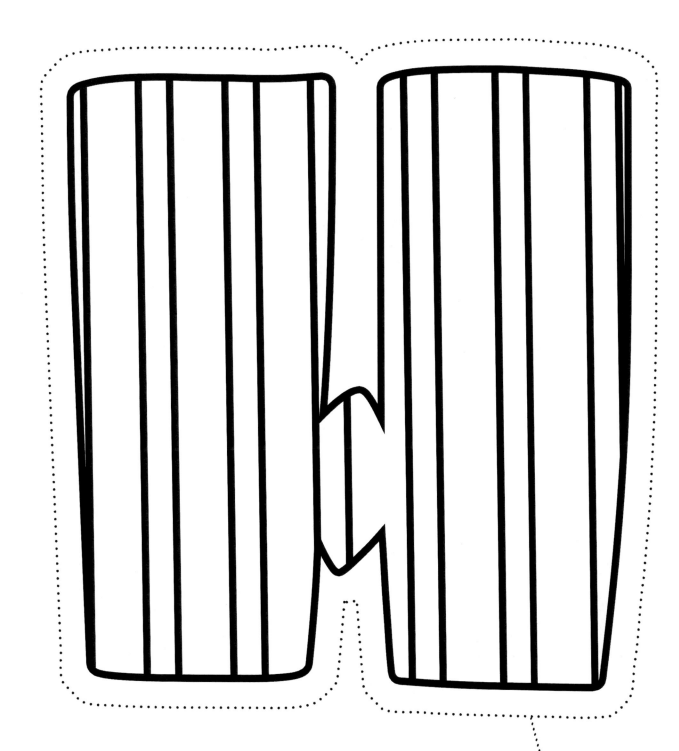

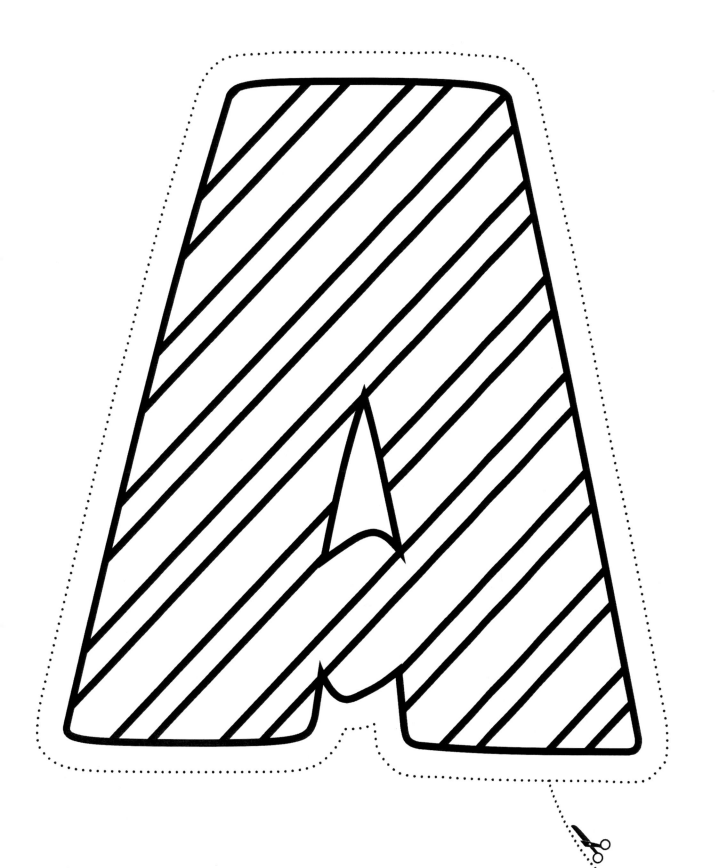

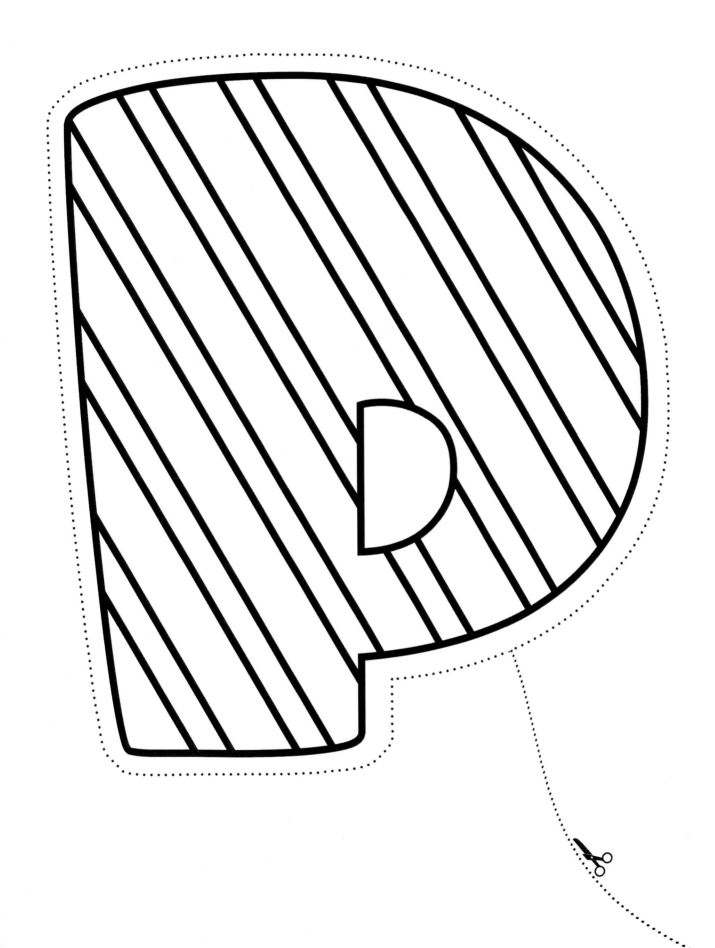

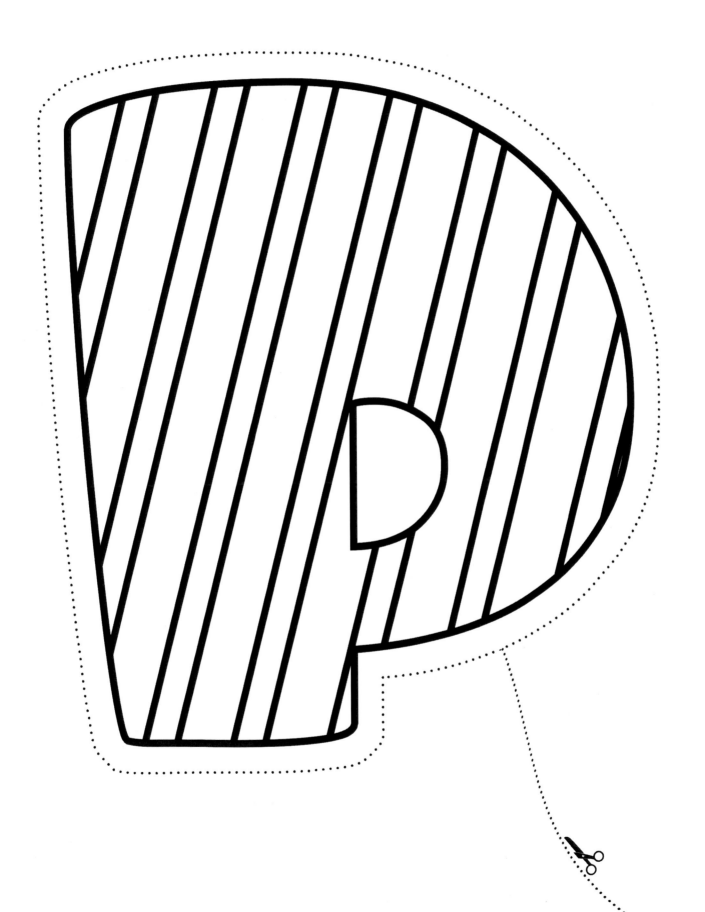

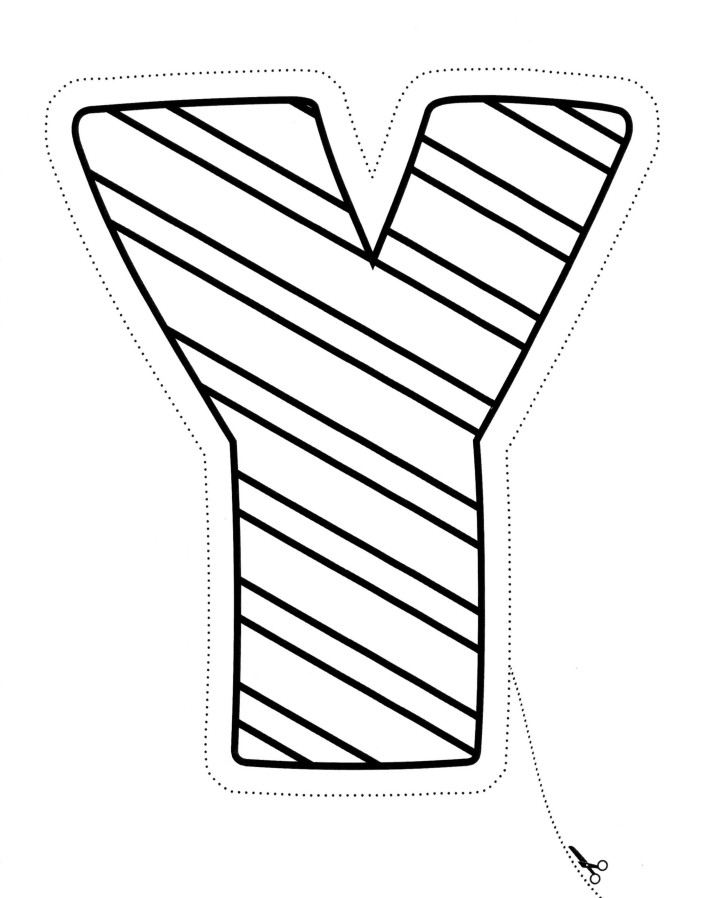

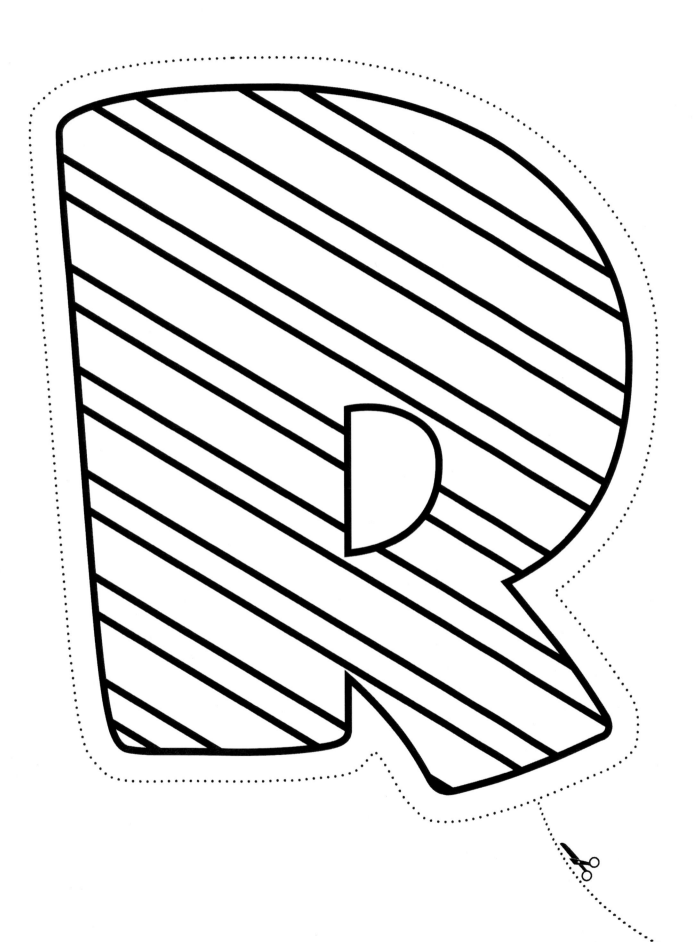

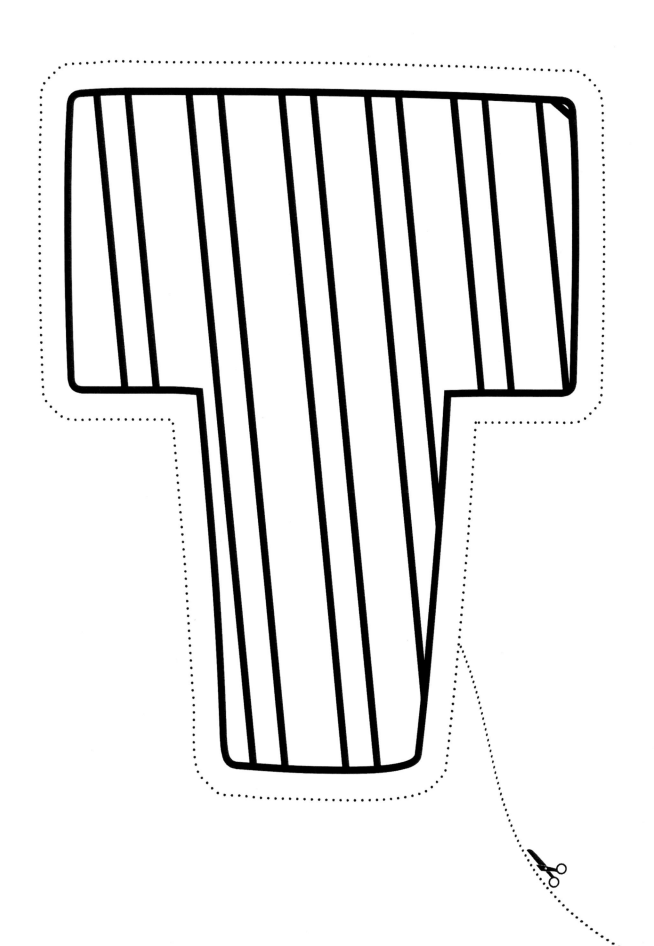

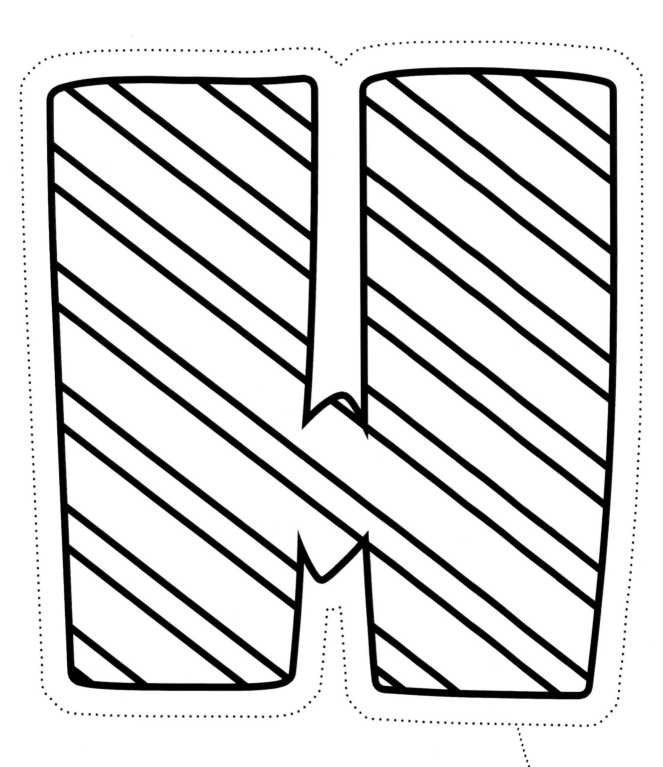

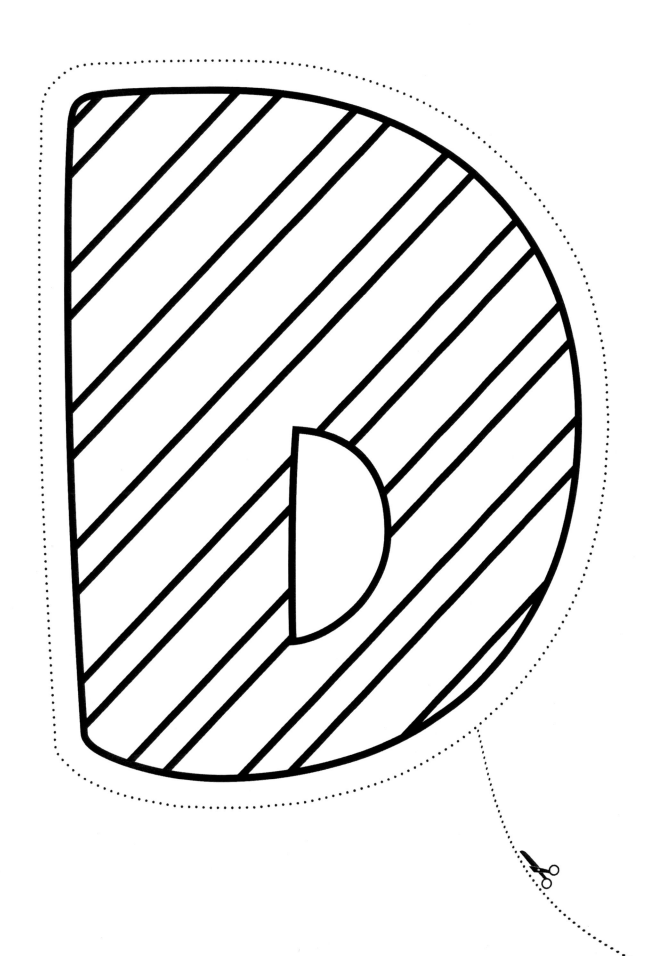

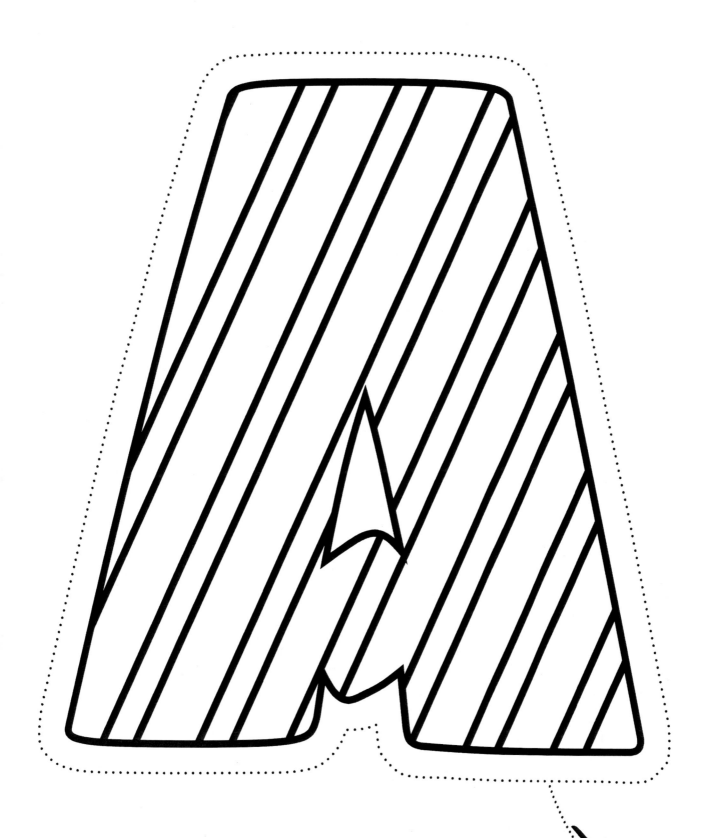

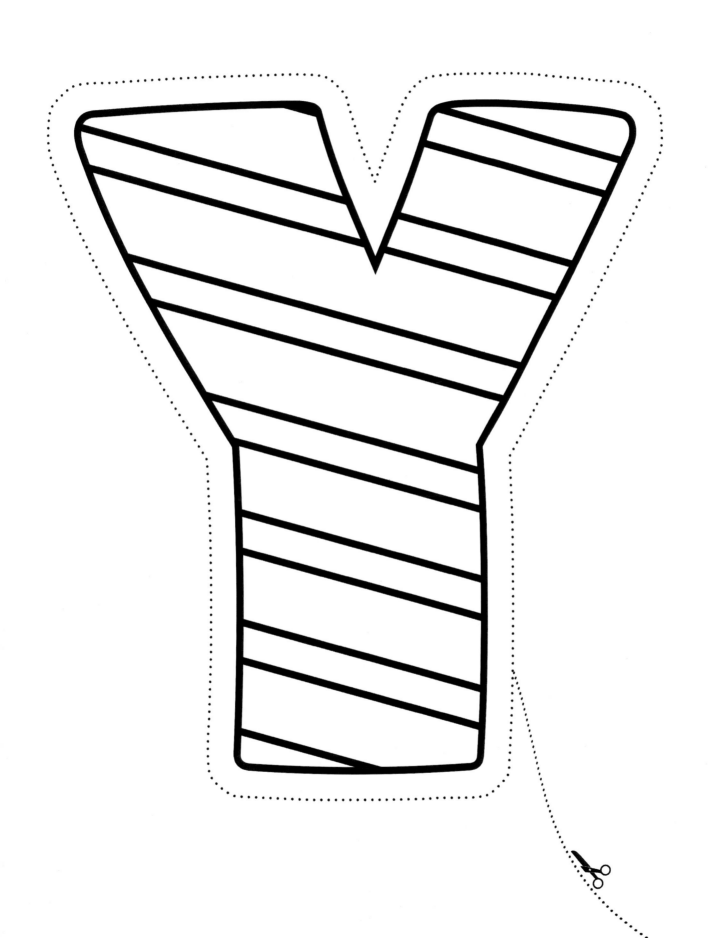

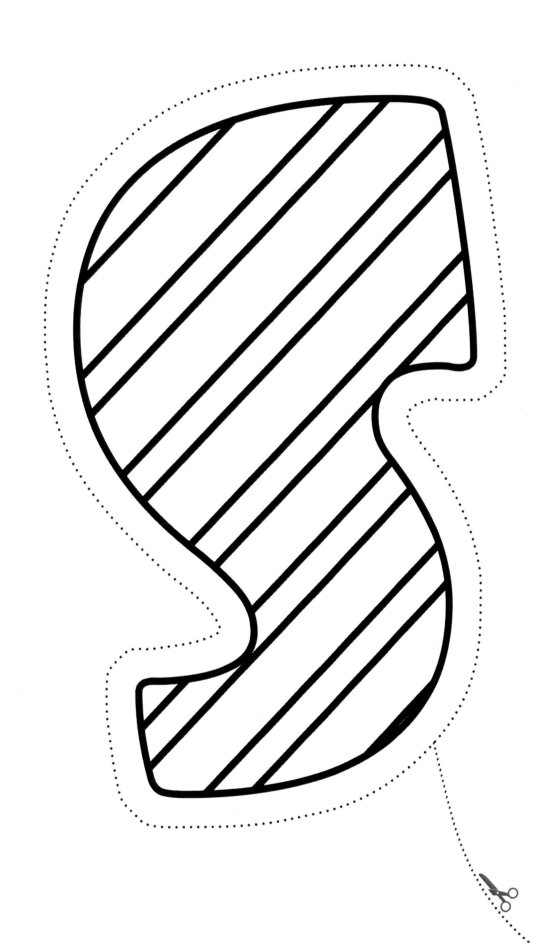

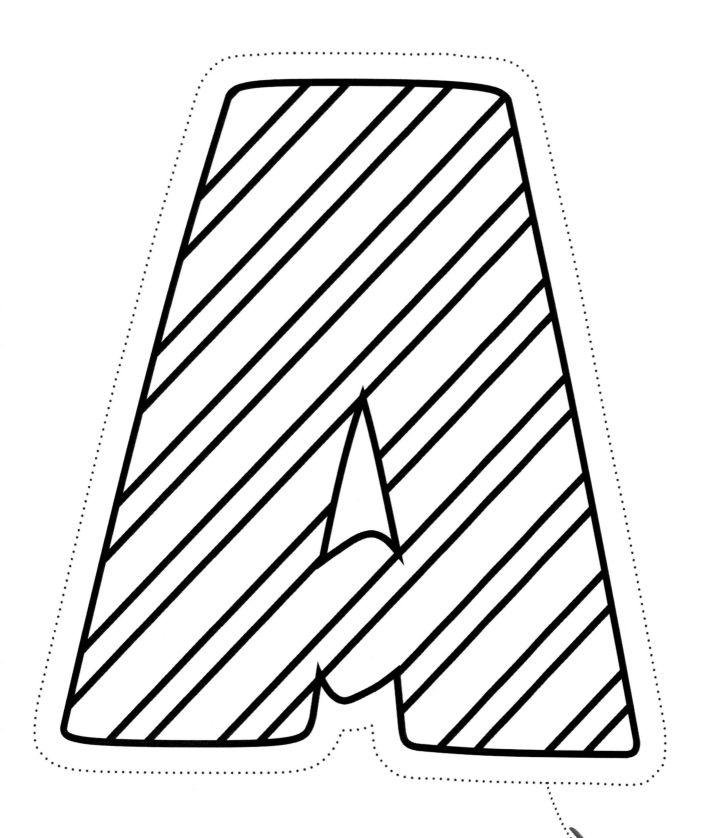

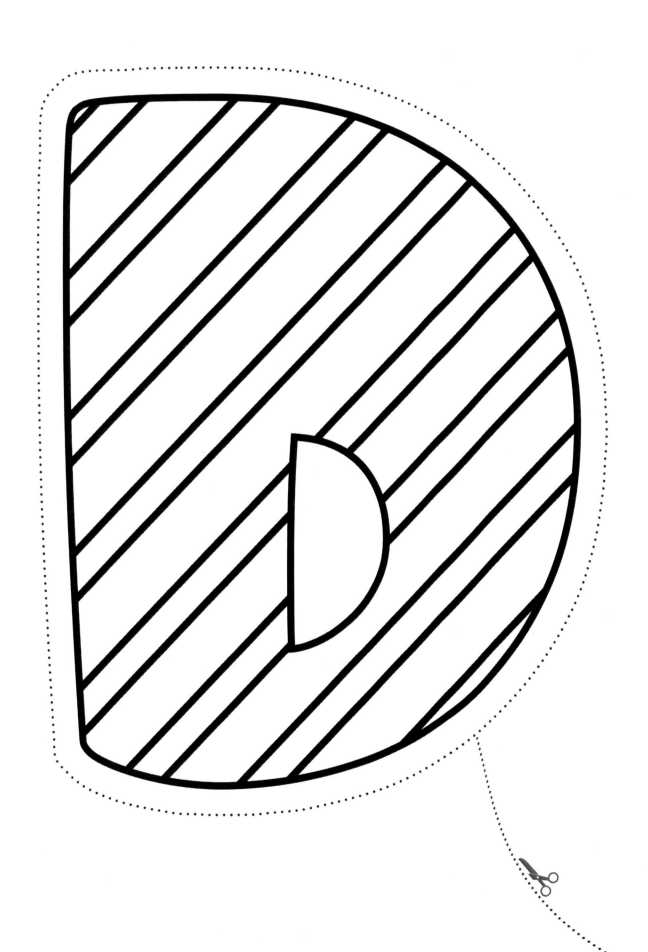

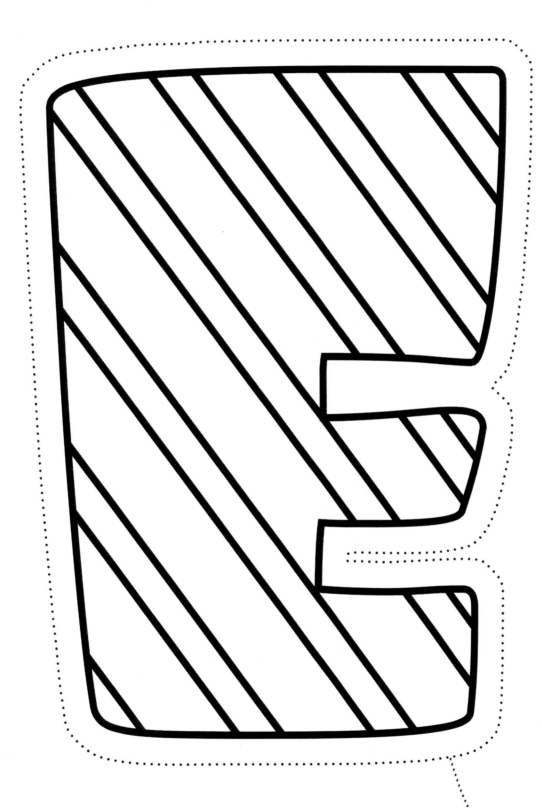

Made in United States
North Haven, CT
16 March 2023

34150618R00041